# MONDO DUPLANTIS

# ATHLETIC JOURNEY

# **FLYING TO GLORY**

Elliot B. Blaze

**Copyright@ 2024 by Elliot B. Blaze**

All rights reserved. No part of this publication may be reproduced, distributed or transmitted in any form or by any means, including photocopying, recording, or other electronic or mechanical methods, without the prior written permission of the publisher, except in the case of brief quotations embodied in critical reviews and certain other noncommercial uses permitted by copyright law.

**Disclaimer**

The following book is for entertainment and informational purposes only. The information presented is without contract or any type of guarantee assurance. While every caution has been taken to provide accurate and current information, it is solely the reader's responsibility to check all information contained in this article before relying upon it. Neither the author nor the publisher can be held accountable for any errors or omissions. Under no circumstances will any legal responsibility or blame be held against the author or publisher for any reparation, damages, or monetary loss due to the information presented, either directly or indirectly. This book is not intended as legal or medical advice. If any such specialized advice is needed, seek a qualified individual for help.

Trademarks are used without permission. Use of the trademark is not authorized by, associated with, or sponsored by the trademark owners. All trademarks and brands used within this book are used with no intent to infringe on the trademark owners and are only used for clarifying purposes.

This book is not sponsored by or affiliated with basketball, its teams, the players, or anyone involved with them.

**Table of Contents**

**INTRODUCTION**
**CHAPTER 1: ROOTS OF A POLE VAULTING PRODIGY**
**CHAPTER 2: BREAKING RECORDS IN THE BACKYARD**
**CHAPTER 3: HIGH SCHOOL HEROICS**
**CHAPTER 4: COLLEGE DREAMS AND DECISIONS**
**CHAPTER 5: RISING ABOVE THE REST**
**CHAPTER 6: THE WORLD RECORD LEAP**
**CHAPTER 7: OLYMPIC GLORY**
**CHAPTER 8: CHALLENGES AND TRIUMPHS**
**CHAPTER 9: THE LIFE OF A CHAMPION**
**CHAPTER 10: LEGACY IN THE MAKING**
**CONCLUSION**

# INTRODUCTION

Few tales shine as brightly as that of Mondo Duplantis in the thrilling world of sports, where every leap, run, and vault is a monument to human potential. "Mondo Duplantis' Athletic Journey: Flying to Glory" is the engrossing story of a young genius who defied expectations and gravity to realize his childhood ambitions instead of merely listing records and championships. This book gives you an inside look at the life of an athlete whose path is both exciting and motivational, taking you from his first steps to his historic accomplishments.

Mondo Duplantis seems destined for greatness right from the start. Mondo was raised in a home where athletics were valued more highly than anything else, and his backyard in Lafayette, Louisiana served as the training ground for his future remarkable athletic career. A child's fun soon gave way to a sight of something much more than that: the extraordinary potential within. The roots of a legend were sown in this serene environment, away from the bright lights of the stadium—a legend that would soon sweep the globe by storm.

Mondo Duplantis was originally exposed to the public by astounding performances that were almost unearthly, a way that few sportsmen can do. He wasn't just removing bars as a teenager—he was shattering barriers in both the real and abstract sense. His uncomplicated climbs, higher than the previous one, enthralled the world of sports. Mondo was more than simply a teenage athlete; he was a budding star who would change the game and become a phenomenon.

It was evident from away that Mondo Duplantis was no typical athlete. He stood out from the crowd due to his innate talent and in-depth knowledge of the pole vaulting craft. He was the young man who always stole the show at social gatherings and who everyone felt was meant for greatness. His early triumphs served as prophecies of things to come rather than just being successes. The world was starting to realize that Mondo was headed for greatness.

And so his path began, characterized as it was by successes but also by an unwavering love for the game. Motivated by a passion for pole vaulting that extended beyond winning medals, Mondo pushed the envelope with each leap. This book follows him on that journey, starting in his backyard vaults and ending in the international arena, where he is still reaching new heights.

"Mondo Duplantis' Athletic Journey: Flying to Glory" celebrates the spirit that propels an athlete to aim for the stars rather than just a sports biography. It's the tale of a young man who inspires us to believe in the strength of perseverance and the excitement of pursuing our dreams with each vault, obstacle, and victory. Turning the pages will reveal not just the emergence of a champion but also the continuing narrative of a legacy being written, one step at a time.

# CHAPTER 1: ROOTS OF A POLE VAULTING PRODIGY

Mondo Duplantis was raised in a family that had a significant influence on his formative years. He was born in Lafayette, Louisiana, on November 10, 1999. The Duplantis family fostered a dynamic atmosphere where athletics and sports were integral parts of everyday existence. But it was more than simply a sports-loving family; it was a family that flourished at developing skills, fostering curiosity, and giving their kids the resources they needed to fully pursue their passions.

Mondo was raised in an environment that was supportive and encouraging from a young age. The Duplantis family was more than just your average American family; they were a unit where individual interests were carefully fostered and aspirations were taken seriously by all members. Greg and Helena, Mondo's parents, were very important in his development. They made sure their kids had access to the greatest environment possible so they could reach their full potential. They were more than just parents; they were mentors, coaches, and facilitators.

Mondo was exposed to a variety of sports and activities as a child. His parents encouraged him to explore a variety of sports and never forced him to stick with one, which helped him develop a passion for physical activity in general. Because of this openness, Mondo was able to form a strong bond with sports at a young age—one that came about organically through play and exploration rather than being coerced.

The backyard served as a playground for Mondo and his siblings to practice and refine their skills, and the Duplantis household was stocked with equipment. Mondo needed this setting to grow since it allowed him to freely explore his potential without feeling pressed for time. The family's strategy was to give the kids the resources they needed and then take a backseat, letting them take the lead in discovering their passions.

Mondo's parents pushed him to have an adventurous spirit and to test limits, traits that characterized his early years. His upbringing was centered on encouraging a love of movement and competitiveness in a lighthearted, encouraging atmosphere rather than on rigorous training schedules or hard coaching from an early age. With this strategy, Mondo was able to grow his athletic abilities naturally and avoided the burnout that can occasionally result from early sports specialization.

Mondo's upbringing was mostly shaped by his family's emotional and psychological support in addition to his physical surroundings. Regardless of whether he was trying something new or honing a talent, his parents were there to support and encourage him. They stressed the value of having fun during the process as opposed to concentrating only on results; this way of thinking helped Mondo keep a positive relationship with sports as he became older.

The Duplantis family raised their kids with a balanced philosophy. Sports were a big part of everyday life, but education, creativity, and personal growth were also highly valued. Mondo was pushed not just to be a great athlete but also to be a well-rounded person with a wide variety of interests. His ability to stay grounded and concentrated was aided by this all-encompassing approach, even as his athletic abilities became more apparent.

Mondo Duplantis's fame as a pole vaulting prodigy has its origins in his family's long sporting heritage. This tradition was more than just a background for him; it was a major influence on how he saw himself and his ability as an athlete. Due to his upbringing in a family rich in sporting history, Mondo was constantly impacted by the successes and life lessons of people around him, which created a special atmosphere where striving for greatness was not only encouraged but practically expected.

The athletic heritage of the Duplantis family is noteworthy. In the 1980s and 1990s, his father, Greg Duplantis, competed at a high level as a pole vaulter in the US. Because of Greg's pole vaulting career, the sport became more than simply a job for him; it also became a daily love for the family. Greg's pole vaulting career introduced Mondo to the sport at a young age and gave him a real-world example of what hard work and discipline in sports could accomplish.

In addition to giving Mondo a role model, Greg's experience as a pole vaulter gave Mondo access to a wealth of information and experience from someone extremely knowledgeable about the nuances of the sport. A foundation that most young athletes lack was established for Mondo by this access to personal information. Mondo inherited Greg's methods, perspectives, and comprehension of the game from an early age; they were ingrained in his approach to athletics. Long before Mondo started his serious athletic career, this link to his father's legacy gave him motivation and a solid technical basis.

In addition to the influence of his father, Mondo was surrounded by other athletes in his family. His mother, Helena Duplantis, née Hedlund, was a successful volleyball player and heptathlete in Sweden. Mondo's upbringing benefited from Helena's athletic experience, which combined the heptathlon's comprehensive approach and the technical demands of pole vaulting. Because of these various influences, Mondo wasn't simply learning about one sport; instead, he was learning about the wider world of athletics and how important it is to be strong, versatile, and well-conditioned in a variety of sports.

Additionally, the Duplantis family was linked to a larger community of sportsmen and enthusiasts. Both of Mondo's older brothers, Andreas and Antoine, were accomplished athletes in their way. Antoine was a baseball player, while Andreas pursued pole vaulting competitively. Because of his siblings' athletic endeavors, he grew up in a family where athletics were important and everyone's accomplishments added to a history of excellence.

Being up in an environment where sports legacy was always present, Mondo was inevitably impacted by the experiences, triumphs, and setbacks of his family members. Mondo was deeply inspired and filled with pride by the sports accomplishments of the Duplantis family. The heritage he received involved more than just carrying on a family custom; it involved holding the flame that previous generations had lighted. A strong sense of purpose and a desire to uphold his family's athletic tradition were instilled in Mondo by this sense of continuity and connection to their past accomplishments.

But this tradition had an impact on Mondo in more ways than just technique or inspiration; it influenced his

14

perception of what it meant to be an athlete. Mondo acquired the virtues of tenacity, fortitude, and the significance of upholding a strong work ethic from the experiences of his mother, father, and siblings. His growth as an athlete was greatly aided by these lessons, which gave him the psychological and emotional fortitude to deal with the demands and hardships of a high-level sports career.

The pivotal events of Mondo Duplantis' early development in the sport—taking his first steps on the runway—mark his journey as a pole vaulting prodigy. These early moves weren't simply physical; they also served as a foundation for his future in pole vaulting and represented the beginning of his potential as a vaulter. From a young age, Mondo came to associate the runway—the place where pole vaulters collect momentum before taking off—with themselves.

The runway in the Duplantis' backyard served as more than just a regular training ground; it was also where Mondo first had contact with pole vaulting. His father, Greg Duplantis, a former pole vaulter, painstakingly built this runway. Mondo was able to participate in the sport in a safe and encouraging setting thanks to the arrangement. This practice space, in contrast to ordinary sporting facilities, was designed with the requirements of an aspiring pole vaulter in mind, giving Mondo a reliable and convenient location to take those crucial initial steps. It was on this precise runway that Mondo first learned the fundamental moves and skills of pole vaulting as a small youngster. During these early sessions, the focus was not just on picking up the sport but also on becoming used to the rhythm and speed that the runway required. Mondo's father worked hard early on to instill in him the sense of time and coordination that are necessary for mastering the runway. To ensure that Mondo understood the significance of each movement, these skills were taught in an age-appropriate manner.

Helping Mondo develop the physical strength and dexterity required to handle the challenges of pole vaulting was another aspect of the early runway focus. This meant, at an early age, engaging in enjoyable but targeted workouts and drills to improve his body control and sprinting speed—two essential components of a successful approach on the runway. Mondo's father made sure that these activities were smoothly incorporated into their training sessions, getting more difficult as Mondo's skills improved.

Mondo had to learn the nuances of body alignment and pole placement in addition to speed during his early runway experiences. His father skillfully assisted him in carrying the pole, emphasizing the value of balance and grasp. This preparatory training on the runway was crucial in assisting Mondo in acquiring the technical accuracy that would eventually define his vaulting style. Mondo used the runway as a venue to continuously hone these abilities until they came naturally to him.

During these initial workouts, Mondo also started to comprehend the mental toughness needed for pole vaulting on the runway. It required concentration and mental clarity to race down the runway, coordinate his motions, and get ready for takeoff. Mondo's early training included a subtle introduction to these concepts, which helped him develop the focus and mental fortitude that are essential for pole vaulting.

The Duplantis family approached these initial stages with support and patience. The emphasis was on laying a strong foundation through practice and positive reinforcement rather than racing to master the technique. Mondo was free to make errors and grow from them, and every time he stepped onto the runway, he became one step closer to understanding the intricacies of the sport.

Mondo's relationship with the runway changed as he grew and changed. He could now come at them farther on the approach, and he could run much faster down the runway. More sophisticated methods were presented by his father, but he always made sure to uphold the fundamental values that were taught in those initial phases. The runway, which was formerly just a piece of land in their backyard, evolved into a hub for Mondo's development.

Mondo had a clear advantage from his early efforts on the runway by the time he started competing in more organized settings. Those early steps under his father's watchful supervision produced comfort with the rhythm, the accuracy of his approach, and the confidence in his ability to manage the pole. All of these things started with that methodical and meticulous practice on that backyard runway, and they would later play a part in Mondo's success on the international scene.

The time that Mondo Duplantis fell in love with pole vaulting is intimately linked to his path as a prodigy. This wasn't a revelation that happened all of a sudden; rather, it was a deep and gradual relationship that developed over time as a result of his curiosity, delight, and unusual upbringing.

Mondo developed a strong love for pole vaulting at a very young age. He was exposed to pole vaulting early on and often since he grew up in an environment where sports were commonplace. Mondo's burgeoning interest in pole vaulting was aided by the equipment, the setup in his backyard, and the regular presence of his father, former pole vaulter Greg Duplantis. But more than simply having access to the necessary equipment, it was about the excitement and delight he had every time he engaged with the pole.

Mondo's childhood attraction to the sport was innately whimsical and inquisitive. He was enthralled by the simple joy of it rather than being instantly focused on mastery or competitiveness. He found that vaulting, the sensation of being in the air, and the difficulty of clearing the bar made for a fun game he wanted to play over and over. Mondo was able to participate in pole vaulting without feeling constrained by expectations or results thanks to this sense of fun. He loved it more the more he vaulted, and this love grew over time into a more intense passion.

Mondo's innate skill and the positive feedback loop it produced also had an impact on his discovery of his affinity for pole vaulting. He showed early on that he was naturally gifted at the sport, with timing and coordination that made it easy for him to pick up new skills. Each vault that went well and each bar that was cleared increased his enthusiasm and devotion to the sport. This encouraging feedback was crucial in transforming what could have been a fleeting interest into a passion that lasted a lifetime.

The sense of achievement Mondo experienced as he started to comprehend and become an expert in the technical facets of pole vaulting was another important component of his growing interest. The intricate sport necessitates a combination of strength, speed, agility, and technique. Mondo found the task of assembling all these components to be thrilling rather than intimidating. He felt a sense of satisfaction and thrill after reaching a new height, which motivated him to keep climbing. What drew him into pole vaulting was, for him, the constant process of learning and progress.

Mondo's family's nurturing atmosphere was also very important in fostering his interest. His parents, in particular his father, encouraged him without exerting undue pressure. They supported Mondo's emerging passion without making it feel like a chore, letting him pursue his interests. With this strategy, Mondo's passion for pole vaulting developed naturally, spurred by his excitement rather than outside influences.

Mondo started devoting more time and effort to pole vaulting as his enthusiasm for the sport grew. What had once been a lighthearted pastime grew to become his life's work. He would practice for hours on end, not because he had to but rather because he enjoyed it. Once a playground, the runway in his backyard served as a location for him to fully immerse himself in the sport he loved. This change signaled a turning point in his life, as his passion started to coincide with a drive to succeed and challenge himself.

Mondo's early competitive experiences served to further cement his devotion. He was never really motivated by winning, but his enjoyment of the game was enhanced by the sense of accomplishment he got from doing well. He could track his development by competing, and the excitement of winning these early competitions strengthened his resolve to pursue pole vaulting. His devotion was rooted in a potent mixture of enjoyment, personal development, and the thrill of competition.

# CHAPTER 2: BREAKING RECORDS IN THE BACKYARD

The pole vaulting accomplishments of Mondo Duplantis throughout his early years are noteworthy not only for their brilliance but also for their unwavering consistency and quick development. His sporting achievements started to mount well before he was thirteen, establishing him as a prodigy with early skill recognition.

Mondo showed a remarkable talent for pole vaulting at the age of four or five, performing actions and feats that were remarkable for someone of that age. While other kids his age were still learning how to use their basic motor abilities, Mondo was experimenting with heights and techniques that were well beyond anything one could have imagined. He cleared heights that were astounding even by the standards of much older athletes thanks to his exceptional mobility and intrinsic mastery of vaulting principles.

As Mondo became bigger, his accomplishments started to show off both his innate talent and his deep commitment to the sport. By the time he was about ten years old, Mondo was always going above and above. Not only was he competing in the pole vault, but he was also setting the standard for others to follow by dominating. His vaulting heights continued to rise, and he started to surpass other young athletes not only in regional and national competitions but also internationally.

Consistently pushing his boundaries was one of Mondo's great childhood accomplishments. In contrast to numerous youthful athletes who may achieve their peak and then stagnate, Mondo consistently achieved new personal records, frequently in rapid succession. His early years were characterized by this unwavering quest for improvement, which showed a degree of focus and drive uncommon in someone so young. Every new height he achieved was not only a record but also evidence of his increasing ability and tenacity.

Mondo's accomplishments during this time were also distinguished by a level of maturity above his years. He performed under pressure with the serenity of an experienced athlete, approaching competitions with a coolness and confidence that belied his youth. He was a fierce competitor even when facing older and more seasoned athletes because of his calm under pressure and physical prowess. His early success was largely due to his ability to cope with the mental demands of pole vaulting at such a young age.

Mondo's early successes in pole vaulting attracted the interest and respect of those involved with the sport. Coaches, players, and fans realized that he was a unique talent and that his achievements weren't just the product of early exposure to the sport or a nurturing atmosphere. Mondo's pole vaulting accomplishments were becoming the standard for future athletes to follow, and his demonstrations were starting to motivate others.

Mondo Duplantis became a pole vaulting prodigy in large part because of the backyard setup in his Duplantis home. This was more than just a training ground; it was a thoughtfully constructed setting meant to develop and polish his abilities from an early age.

Mondo's father, Greg Duplantis, was a former pole vaulter, and he is the source of the backyard pole vault arrangement. Recognizing the value of having a reliable and convenient practice space, Greg constructed a pole vaulting field in their Lafayette, Louisiana backyard. This wasn't simply a basic set-up; it was a scaled-down representation of the professional runways and vaulting sections seen in sports arenas. It has landing mats, a box where the pole is planted, and a runway, all designed for a young athlete just beginning to learn the sport.

The amount of thought and detail that went into building the backyard arrangement was what set it apart. Greg made sure the runway surface resembled those used in contests so Mondo could experience and feel like he was in a professional setting. Young vaulters are particularly concerned about the possibility of injury, so Mondo can train without it thanks to the thoughtful construction of the landing space and pole vault box.

One important element in Mondo's quick development was the setup's proximity to his house. Mondo could practice anytime he wanted, without being restricted by set training times or needing to use a public facility, because it was right outside his door. Because of this ease, he was able to interact with the sport in his own way and experiment at his own speed with various methods and strategies. Mondo used the backyard set-up as his private playground to immerse himself in the principles of pole vaulting, frequently spending hours honing his technique.

Furthermore, the arrangement was flexible enough to accommodate Mondo's development as a player. The runway length could be changed and the bar could be raised to correspond with his growing skill level as he grew older. Because of its adaptability, the setting remained demanding and pertinent, fostering Mondo's growth throughout the entirety of his early career.

Another important factor in Mondo's mental and emotional attachment to pole vaulting was the backyard arrangement. Pole vaulting became more than just something he accomplished at a distant facility; it became an essential part of his everyday life because it was in his backyard. The sport was always present in his surroundings, which contributed to his strong familiarity and comfort level with the vaulting technique. Mondo first discovered his love for the game in the garden, where he could practice without fear of failure and gain the self-assurance that would eventually catapult him to worldwide recognition.

The astounding juvenile records he set at an extraordinarily young age are the most notable markers of his quest to break records in the backyard. These records were as more than just benchmarks; they served as evidence of his extraordinary talent and high degree of proficiency, which he displayed even before he reached adolescence.

Mondo was doing more than simply pole vaulting at a young age; he was reaching heights that other young sportsmen could only imagine. He started breaking the first of his numerous youth records in the backyard since it offered him a reliable area to train and test his abilities. These records were noteworthy because, in addition to being local or national records, they were frequently world records for his age group, proving that Mondo was not only better than his American counterparts but also better than anyone on the globe.

The constancy with which Mondo set the bar for his early records was one of their most important features. He was frequently shattering his records as a young child, frequently in fast succession. This was the outcome of his incredible dedication to honing his skills and raising his vaulting heights, not only of natural growth and development. With each new record, he demonstrated his physical prowess and in-depth knowledge of the sport, marking a major advancement in his abilities.

When Mondo was just seven years old, he set his first noteworthy child record, reaching heights that were remarkable for someone so young. Other records quickly followed this early one as Mondo kept improving his strength and technique. He began vaulting at heights that were unusual for his age group by the time he was nine or 10 years old. Even while these records were frequently established during unofficial practice sessions in his backyard, that didn't make them any less important. Mondo's status as a young athlete with exceptional potential was established by the meticulous documentation and verification of each record.

Mondo's record-breaking feats increased in magnitude as he approached his preteen years. He started to go beyond what was thought to be feasible for a vaulter of his age, frequently clearing heights several feet higher than prior marks held by other young vaulters. The pole vaulting community took notice of Mondo's ability to continuously set new marks and realized that he was doing something unique.

The improvement he showed was just as important as the heights he reached when setting these youth records. Mondo's record-breaking was part of a clear and consistent progression, in contrast to many young athletes who might have occasional accomplishments. The rigorous work he put into perfecting the sport was reflected in each new record he set, which was part of a bigger trend of growth and advancement. The records became landmarks in his quest, each one serving as a springboard for even bigger successes.

Even after Mondo advanced to more competitive levels of competition, his youth records frequently went uncontested for years, which made them noteworthy as well. These records raised the bar for what was possible for young pole vaulters and established a new benchmark. Other young athletes were motivated by Mondo's achievements to work harder and set greater goals since they saw that remarkable things could be accomplished at an early age.

Mondo Duplantis' early career was defined by the turning point when the world began to take notice of him. It was at this point that he went from being a highly skilled young athlete to a globally recognized prodigy. This crucial event wasn't at a huge championship or in a lavish stadium; rather, it was based on the incredible accomplishments he made in his own backyard.

As Mondo kept setting new milestones and reaching unheard-of heights for his age, word got out beyond his neighborhood. At first, the child who was seemingly effortless in his height clearances piqued the interest of pole vaulting fans and smaller athletic circles. However as Mondo's accomplishments increased in frequency and stature, the focus grew to include a far wider audience.

The center of this increasing interest was the backyard setup, where Mondo perfected his craft and broke records. As videos of Mondo vaulting in his backyard began to circulate online, the world of athletics was captivated. The mix of his youth, skill, and the laid-back setting in which he was accomplishing these feats was just as impressive as the height of his vaults in these movies. People thought it remarkable and inspirational to watch a little youngster vault at world-class standards in a backyard environment.

Mondo accomplished a vault in one of these backyard practices that genuinely caught the attention of the entire world. This particular vault was noteworthy even for much older competitors; it was not just another youth record. The video from this vault went viral very fast on social media and sports networks, making Mondo a household name. All of a sudden, experts and pundits worldwide were talking about this little child from Lafayette, Louisiana, as a possible future sports star.

Media attention spiked at the same time that the globe started to pay attention. Sports analysts and journalists started contacting this young prodigy to find out more information. News organizations and big sports journals began to feature interviews with Mondo and his family. People were drawn in and impressed by the tale of the young man who was setting records in his backyard. The world was unable to overlook the captivating story that Mondo's young excitement, extraordinary talent, and modest setting of his accomplishments created.

For Mondo, this widespread recognition marked a sea change. Opportunities for increased visibility and competition on a bigger platform came with it. As invitations to worldwide contests and exhibits started to come in, Mondo found himself moving from backyard vaults to arenas full of onlookers. Because of the global attention, Mondo's pole vaulting career was now in jeopardy, with expectations rising in tandem with his increasing notoriety.

# CHAPTER 3: HIGH SCHOOL HEROICS

Mondo Duplantis was a standout athlete long before he started his professional career. His tremendous dominance in the pole vaulting arena defined his high school years. Mondo, a Louisiana native who attended Lafayette High School, rose to prominence fast in high school sports, especially in the pole vaulting competition where he often outperformed his colleagues.

It was evident from the start of high school that Mondo was not just another gifted athlete—rather, he was extraordinary. He was able to overcome obstacles that most high school players could only imagine thanks to his training, which was refined over years of immersion in an athletic environment. Mondo had already achieved competitive heights by his sophomore year, not only in high school but also in undergraduate competitions. He distinguished himself from his rivals with his ability to routinely clear ever-higher bars, and he soon became the athlete to watch at every meet.

Mondo gave some truly amazing performances in his high school career. He frequently broke his records numerous times in a single season, smashing both school-wide and personal marks. His defining quality was his ability to perform under duress, especially in championship meets. Mondo's high school career served as evidence of his extraordinary talent and commitment in a sport where consistency is crucial. His vaults demonstrated force, accuracy, and technical proficiency which was surprising given his youth.

Mondo's unwavering quest for greatness during his high school years was what made him stand out. He had a reputation for working himself to the absolute extent to get every edge and refine his technique. His hard work paid off, as he routinely gave excellent performances and frequently prevailed by wide margins. He became a legend in the local sports community because of his dominance, which did not cease after one season but continued throughout his high school career.

Intense competition characterized Mondo's high school years, as he frequently competed against older, more seasoned athletes. He routinely excelled in them despite this, displaying an unusual level of maturity and poise for someone his age. One of the fundamental reasons for his domination was his capacity to stay composed and concentrated under pressure. Whether it was a state championship or a local meet, Mondo consistently performed to the amazement of his rivals.

Mondo's performance at the Louisiana High School Athletic Association (LHSAA) state championships was one of the highlights of his high school career. Here, he often outperformed the opposition, creating new state marks and solidifying his place among the nation's best high school pole vaulters. Huge audiences flocked to see him vault, and his performances were frequently the event's high point. Mondo's ability to draw attention at these events was a direct reflection of his potential to become a top-tier athlete in the future.

Beyond simply winning, Mondo's supremacy in high school pole vaulting redefined what was feasible at that caliber. His ability to reach heights previously believed to be unreachable by a high school athlete redefined the bar for success in the sport. Coaches and teammates agreed that they were seeing something unique in this athlete who was deliberately pushing the limits of the sport rather than merely playing it.

A teenager participating in a sport as specialized as pole vaulting rarely garners as much national and international attention as Mondo Duplantis did during his high school years. His outstanding high school accomplishments soon spread beyond Louisiana, piqueing the interest of the international athletic world as well as the national media.

Mondo's incredible record-breaking jumps, which were competitive with elite athletes worldwide in addition to being impressive locally, marked the beginning of his meteoric climb in the pole vaulting world. Not unnoticed, as a high school student, he was consistently clearing heights that matched those of seasoned pros. Major sports publications started to take notice of him when he excelled in several national tournaments. They were amazed by the young prodigy who seemed to come out of nowhere and have the ability to break records.

After Mondo started breaking records for high school seniors nationwide, the media began to focus more on him. Sports journalists frequently praised his accomplishments and made predictions about his future in the game. Since foreign athletics organizations acknowledged his record-breaking performances, this attention went beyond American borders. Talk about pole vaulting's future began to mention Mondo, with many speculating that he would one day rank among the sport's greatest.

Mondo received invites to participate in renowned competitions that were usually only extended to older, more seasoned sportsmen as a result of his growing reputation. He was able to compete in these top events even while he was still in high school, frequently placing close to the top and enhancing his reputation as a rising talent. Even among the elite in the sport, Mondo's participation in these tournaments demonstrated that he was regarded as a serious contender.

Among the most important turning points in Mondo's high school career was when he started competing abroad. His accomplishments on the international scene drew much attention, and he soon established himself as one of the world's most promising young sportsmen. Mondo competed against more experienced, professional vaulters and continually produced amazing scores, proving he was more than just a high school sensation but also a genuine talent on the global stage.

The media craze surrounding Mondo was further stoked by his success abroad. His accomplishments received widespread media coverage, with headlines hailing his extraordinary talent and promise. Coaches, athletes, and spectators from all over the world started to take notice as well, realizing that Mondo was not just the pole vaulting sport's future but also one that was already having a big influence on it.

Mondo had to live up to the hype in addition to the attention he received. He did, however, appear to enjoy the attention, taking it as fuel to keep getting better and pushing the boundaries of what was thought to be achievable for a high school athlete. His maturity and mental toughness, which further won him over to critics and fans alike, demonstrated his ability to bear pressure and perform on the highest platforms.

For any student-athlete, juggling school and sports may be difficult, but for Mondo Duplantis, it was especially difficult because of the level of competition he played. Even though Mondo had achieved remarkable success in pole vaulting, he was still a high school student with the same obligations to his studies as his classmates. It took rigorous time management, self-control, and encouragement from his family and school to balance these competing demands.

Mondo went to Lafayette High School in Louisiana, where he was well-known for his dedication to his education in addition to his athletic ability. Even though his pole vaulting career was rapidly gaining momentum, Mondo recognized the significance of keeping a strong academic background. Mondo's parents, Greg and Helena Duplantis made sure he didn't skip school despite his hectic training and competition schedule by emphasizing the importance of education.

For Mondo in his high school years, a typical day was everything but typical. His days had to be carefully organized to balance exercise and education. Mondo had to be a time-manager; he frequently got up early to finish his schoolwork before going to practice. His afternoons were usually devoted to training or competition, which left little time for his ordinary high school schedule. Mondo didn't let this deter him from concentrating on his studies since he knew that performance in the classroom was just as vital as performance on the field.

Teachers and administrators at Mondo's school were cognizant of his special circumstances and offered assistance to enable him to balance his two roles. They collaborated with him to make sure he could continue his education and pursue his sports career. This frequently meant adjusting his competition travel schedule, letting him finish projects from a distance, or offering more assistance when he needed it to catch up. To balance his academics and athletics, Mondo needed the support of this network.

Apart from the administrative difficulties involved in managing his studies and athletic career, Mondo also had to cope with the psychological and emotional stress of playing two different characters. Athletes sometimes face extreme physical and mental strain while competing at a high level; this pressure is compounded when

41

juggling academic obligations. Nonetheless, Mondo was able to overcome these obstacles thanks to his innate discipline and strong work ethic, which he developed at a young age. He gained knowledge on stress management, task prioritization, and organization—skills that would come in handy in his professional life.

Mondo continued to be a committed student despite the pressures of his sports career. His remarkable performance in both domains bears witness to his unwavering commitment and robust work ethic. He realized that his education could support and further his growth as a well-rounded person rather than being something that had to be sacrificed for his athletic career. Throughout his high school career, Mondo was able to succeed both academically and athletically thanks to this well-rounded approach.

A major turning point in Mondo Duplantis' athletic career was his decision to become a full-fledged professional pole vaulter, having previously competed as a recognized high school athlete. This was not an easy choice to make; it required balancing the normal path of pursuing collegiate competition and studying against the possibility of a bright future in athletics.

As Mondo's high school career developed, the international athletic community started to take notice of his pole vaulting accomplishments. He was performing at a level well above that of most athletes his age by the time he was approaching the end of his high school career. Mondo had previously broken several records and outperformed the average high school or even collegiate athlete in competition. Due to his remarkable achievement, there were talks about going professional, which would enable him to compete against the world's best and devote all of his attention to his pole vaulting career.

The realization that Mondo was already among the sport's best due to his talent and accomplishments had a significant role in his choice to become a professional. Staying in the amateur ranks would have required him to compete in a system that was no longer able to properly test or develop his skills. He would be able to compete on a global scale, work with elite trainers, have access to state-of-the-art training facilities, and obtain sponsorships to help him achieve his sporting goals if he turned professional.

The possibility of achieving financial security that came with becoming a professional was another important consideration in this choice. Mondo would be able to make money as a professional athlete through sponsorships, endorsements, and prize money. Not only did he need this money for competition and training, but it also allowed him to concentrate fully on his athletic career without having to worry about money. Going pro was an attractive option for him since it would let him pursue his love for a living, especially given the considerable expenses involved in competing at the highest levels of the sport.

His family's guidance and support, who were well-versed in the sports industry, also had an impact on his choice. Mondo received invaluable guidance from his father, Greg Duplantis, a former high-level pole vault competitor when making decisions. Mondo gained important insights into the realities of a professional sports career from his family's athletic background, which enabled him to see the chances and difficulties that were ahead.

Mondo ultimately decided to become a professional because he wanted to challenge himself and take on the world's greatest athletes. He realized that his development and potential would have been constrained had he remained in the amateur ranks. Mondo was able to devote all of his time and effort to becoming the greatest pole vaulter he could be by turning professional. This choice also demonstrated his willingness to assume the duties and demands of being a professional athlete, where there are greater standards for performance and more intense rivalry.

# CHAPTER 4: COLLEGE DREAMS AND DECISIONS

Mondo Duplantis' choice to continue his education at Louisiana State University (LSU) represented a turning point in both his scholastic and athletic career. Several considerations, including his preferences and the benefits the university offered, played a role in his decision to attend LSU.

Mondo's ties to Louisiana played a major role in his decision to commit to LSU. Mondo found LSU to be an attractive alternative because he was familiar with the local way of life and culture having grown up in Lafayette, Louisiana. Because of his proximity to home, he was able to take advantage of the opportunities provided by a prominent university while still having a solid support network of family and friends.

Another important consideration for Mondo was LSU's well-known track and field program. With its track record of success in track and field, the university offered a high caliber of coaching and competition. Mondo was drawn to the opportunity to play in a reputable program and train with knowledgeable instructors since it gave him the ability to advance his abilities while maintaining a high standard of competition.

Mondo was able to participate in collegiate athletics at LSU thanks to the NCAA program, which provided an atmosphere that was distinct from that of high school or the workplace. He was able to work in a collaborative setting that was both competitive and encouraging at LSU with a group of coaches and athletes who were committed to excellence. The resources and facilities of the university were built to accommodate elite training, which was necessary for Mondo to keep improving as a pole vaulter.

Mondo was able to pursue his scholastic goals in addition to his athletic ones because of LSU. LSU's academic-athletic balance was designed to help student-athletes successfully manage their two duties. Mondo was able to continue success in all areas by focusing on his schoolwork and pursuing his athletic aspirations in this atmosphere.

Mondo Duplantis left his mark on the collegiate athletics scene during his time at Louisiana State University (LSU), where he was known for his outstanding accomplishments in contests. A string of outstanding performances throughout his tenure at LSU not only demonstrated his potential but also cemented his status as one of the sport's most promising young pole vaulters.

Mondo became a dominant force in collegiate pole vaulting as soon as he joined the LSU Tigers. He immediately and significantly changed the NCAA by setting new performance criteria. His exceptional consistency in clearing tall hurdles set him apart from the competition at multiple college events, drawing admiration from spectators and fellow competitors.

Mondo had nothing less than outstanding results in NCAA tournaments. He participated in several competitions and titles, always achieving excellent outcomes. He demonstrated his pole vaulting prowess and technique by clearing bars at heights that were frequently unheard of for a collegiate athlete. Mondo's ability to perform to a high quality during the college season was evidence of his hard work and preparedness.

A memorable experience during Mondo's collegiate tenure was his involvement in the NCAA Championships. He showed off his extraordinary talent at these esteemed competitions by turning in strong performances and frequently topping the leaderboard. The athletics community eagerly awaited his efforts, as his victory in the NCAA Championships solidified his status as one of the nation's top pole vaulters.

Throughout his undergraduate career, Mondo broke numerous records. He demonstrated his ability to push the limits of what was feasible in collegiate pole vaulting by setting new NCAA records. In addition to their technical prowess, his record-breaking vaults were praised for their historical significance to collegiate athletics. Mondo's accomplishments increased awareness of the sport of pole vaulting and raised the prestige of LSU's track and field department.

Mondo's performances were always marked by a great degree of control and precision during his time at LSU. His ability to perform with exceptional precision and refinement allowed him to clear heights that many of his rivals could not match. His reputation as one of the best collegiate athletes was cemented by this caliber of play, which also hinted at his future greatness.

Mondo's participation in collegiate leagues affected the sport more broadly. His accomplishments raised awareness of collegiate pole vaulting and demonstrated the skill and potential available at the collegiate level. His accomplishments inspired other sportsmen and added to the developing interest in pole vaulting as a competitive sport.

During his time as a student at Louisiana State University (LSU), Mondo Duplantis had tremendous progress, characterized by both early setbacks and noteworthy victories. Mondo had several challenges as he made the move from high school to college that put his abilities, flexibility, and fortitude to the test. His approach to training and competition was greatly influenced by these early setbacks, which eventually resulted in a string of victories that showcased his extraordinary talent.

Mondo was confronted with a new standard of expectations and competition when he arrived at LSU. Compared to high school, college athletics offered a different set of demands, especially at a program as competitive as LSU. The level of competition from other collegiate athletes was higher, and training sessions were held more frequently and with greater intensity. It took some time for Mondo to get used to this new setting as she adjusted to the demands of collegiate pole vaulting.

Mondo's first adjustment to the new coaching philosophy and training program at LSU was one of the difficulties he encountered. Even though he was already quite successful in high school, collegiate training programs take a different approach, emphasizing technical refinement and strategy adaptation. Mondo had to work with the LSU coaching staff to adjust to these changes and incorporate their training regimen, which called for adaptability and a desire to pick up new skills.

A new hurdle that came with moving to college was juggling athletics and academics. For Mondo, juggling an intense workout regimen with his academic obligations required a big adjustment. Careful time management and the capacity to focus both on and off the track were necessary for this balancing act. Mondo was able to bear the strains of college life because of his commitment to both his education and his sport, even in the face of these demands.

Despite these difficulties, Mondo had several noteworthy victories in his early undergraduate career that demonstrated his extraordinary skills. His early college meet performances made it clear that he had talent and promise beyond high school. Mondo's ability to achieve remarkable heights during his rookie season demonstrated his athleticism and technical skill, paving the way for a fruitful collegiate career.

Record-breaking performances were one of Mondo's early victories. His skill and training paid off as he broke several collegiate records. These records not only demonstrated his extraordinary skill but also made him a well-known name in college pole vaulting. His accomplishments raised awareness of his career and established a high bar for subsequent performances.

An additional noteworthy achievement was Mondo's performance at the NCAA Championships. He overcame the early difficulties to produce exceptional performances that helped him place first in these renowned competitions. His potential and tenacity were evident in his ability to perform well under the stress of a national tournament. Mondo's standing as one of the best pole vaulters in college was cemented by his performance at the NCAA Championships.

Mondo's achievements were also demonstrated by his capacity to bounce back from early disappointments and hone his craft. He approached every obstacle he encountered with the determination to get better, which resulted in ongoing growth and success. He showed his tenacity and devotion to his sport by tackling and conquering these challenges.

Mondo Duplantis saw a turning point in his career when he went from playing collegiate athletics at Louisiana State University (LSU) to competing internationally. This period was characterized by notable advancements in both his professional trajectory and athletic performance. This entailed making the adjustment from the cutthroat world of undergraduate athletics to the fiercely competitive world of international sports, where the stakes were higher and the competition level more intense.

When Mondo graduated from college, he faced a new set of chances and challenges as he entered the working world. Global competition meant going up against some of the world's top athletes, each with a unique competitive advantage and well-established track record. Mondo had to adjust to new competition formats, increased performance standards, and the demands of representing himself as a professional athlete during the shift.

Adjusting to a higher level of competition was a crucial part of this shift. In contrast to undergraduate competitions, where competitors might have varied in experience and ability, the world stage included seasoned pros who had developed their skills through years of intense competition. Mondo had to hone his strategy, concentrating on mental toughness and maximum performance to contend with such a strong field.

A calculated approach to career management and international reputation development was required when he entered the professional circuit. Mondo had to adjust to the demands of the professional circuit, which included taking part in several international events, attending professional training camps, and fulfilling endorsement obligations. The increased range of tasks necessitated meticulous preparation and setting of priorities to harmonize his sporting achievements with the commercial facets of a professional job.

Important occasions like the World Championships and the Diamond League series served as a catalysts for Mondo's introduction into international competition. An international audience watched and studied his performances in these esteemed meets with great interest. Mondo had to compete at such prestigious events and always give his best as every tournament could affect his rating and prospects.

Public scrutiny and media attention surged when the world stage was reached. Mondo had to deal with the psychological strain of being a great athlete in a highly visible sport in addition to the physical demands of competition. Managing the media, public expectations, and performance pressure necessitated resilience and a laser-like focus. Mondo's success in making the shift from college to the international scene depended heavily on his capacity to remain calm and concentrated in the face of these challenges.

Mondo's collegiate experiences and support networks were invaluable during this shift. His time at LSU gave him a strong intellectual and athletic foundation, giving him the tools he needed to succeed in the working world. As he transitioned into international competition, his family, collegiate coaches, and mentorship provided invaluable support.

# CHAPTER 5: RISING ABOVE THE REST

The way Mondo Duplantis performed in his first international events had a big impact on his rise to prominence in the pole vaulting world. These early international experiences gave him the chance to show off his skills and leave a lasting impression on the sport, laying the groundwork for his future professional career.

Mondo fought seasoned competitors from all over the world in several major competitions, which marked the beginning of his international career. His presence and ability to compete at the top levels of the sport were established during these early international events.

Birmingham, England hosted the 2018 IAAF World Indoor Championships, one of Mondo's first major international competitions. He made an amazing start at this competition, clearing 5.90 meters to win a silver medal. This performance was important because it demonstrated his potential and established him as a young athlete with promise in the world of pole vaulting. His performance in this competition offered compelling evidence of his ability to compete at the greatest levels.

Mondo then took part in the World Championships in Doha, Qatar, in 2019. He won the gold medal in this tournament after achieving a height of 6.05 meters, demonstrating his continuous impressive accomplishments. This accomplishment was noteworthy because it demonstrated his ability to perform well in important international competitions and made him known as one of the world's best pole vaulters. Gaining the gold medal at such a renowned competition was a significant turning point in his career and confirmed his standing internationally.

Mondo's technical skill and capacity to execute well in high-stakes situations were hallmarks of his early international tournament success. His performance in these competitions proved he was prepared to compete at the highest levels of the sport and paved the way for his future successes.

Competing against the finest athletes in the world has been a defining feature of Mondo Duplantis' rise in pole vaulting. His status as a top athlete in the sport has been established by his ability to perform at elite international competitions.

Mondo participated in high-profile competitions early in his career, facing off against some of the world's best pole vaulters. These contests were essential for putting his abilities to the test against the top players in the industry and presenting his brilliance to a global audience.

Mondo repeatedly faced the best opponents in the sport at competitions like the World Championships and the Diamond League series, showcasing his skill in it. Competing against athletes who were well-known personalities in the pole vaulting world, his accomplishments in these meets were a credit to his ability and training.

It was evident from Mondo's ability to compete successfully against these elite vaulters both his remarkable technical prowess and competitive edge. He faced opponents who were seasoned in elite competition, so every meeting was a fresh challenge. His performance in these conditions demonstrated his ability to perform well among the top pole vaulters in the world.

In addition to his technical prowess and competition accomplishments, Mondo Duplantis' ascension in pole vaulting has been marked by his capacity to manage the tremendous strain and expectations that come with being a top athlete in the sport. Given his early triumphs and the attention he received as a prodigious talent, Mondo had great expectations from the beginning of his career.

Mondo had a lot of pressure to live up to the hype when he made the move from high school to the international scene. Expectations were rapidly raised by his performances in important international competitions, as supporters, coaches, and experts expected him to continue dominating. The prominence and attention that come with competing at the top levels of athletics, when every performance is carefully observed and evaluated, added to this pressure.

Keeping up a high standard of performance while handling the pressure of being a top contender was the difficult part of managing these expectations. Mondo had to balance the demands of public scrutiny and media attention with delivering outcomes regularly. To handle the psychological components of competing in this setting, a strong mental focus was just as important as physical preparation.

Mondo used a combination of strategic planning and mental toughness to manage the pressure. He collaborated extensively with sports psychologists and coaches to create strategies for staying calm under duress. This included keeping his attention on the competition process rather than the final result, which helped him remain realistic and control the tension brought on by having high expectations.

His network of support was essential in assisting him in overcoming the demands of his line of work. He received the support and direction he needed from his teammates, coaches, and family to maintain his focus and give his best effort. It was thanks to this network of support that Mondo was able to manage outside pressures and keep a balanced view of his job.

Mondo Duplantis' ascent to prominence in the pole vaulting world has been characterized by several pivotal events that have shaped his career and solidified his place among the sport's elite vaulters. These incidents demonstrate not only his physical prowess but also his capacity to perform well in the spotlight of international competition.

A major turning point in Mondo's history occurred at the 2019 World Championships in Doha, Qatar. He won the gold medal in this competition with a historic triumph, clearing a height of 6.05 meters. This achievement was noteworthy for several reasons: it not only gave him the top rank but also proved that he could compete with the best vaulters in the world at the highest level. His personal best clearance of 6.05 meters demonstrated his extraordinary skill and preparation, making him a notable performer in the world of pole vaulting.

At the Tokyo Olympics in 2020, there was yet another crucial occasion. Even though the COVID-19 epidemic forced the event to take place in 2021, it was a pivotal moment for Mondo. He made a spectacular display in Tokyo, clearing 6.02 meters to win the gold. This accomplishment was especially noteworthy since it demonstrated his ability to execute at the highest level at the most important international sporting event and confirmed his position as an exceptional pole vaulter.

At the 2021 World Indoor Championships in Belgrade, Serbia, Mondo also made news. He vaulted 6.19 meters during this competition, setting a new indoor world record. His career was defined by this record-breaking effort, which demonstrated both his technical prowess and his capacity to push the limits of the sport. His remarkable talent and ability to compete at the top of his game in competitive settings were demonstrated by his record.

Another significant turning point in his career occurred at the Eugene, Oregon, 2022 World Championships, where he won the gold medal and once again proved his mettle. Several outstanding vaults contributed to his triumph, which cemented his standing as one of the world's best pole vaulters. This effort strengthened his standing as a prominent player in the sport and added to his expanding list of accomplishments.

# CHAPTER 6: THE WORLD RECORD LEAP

Mondo Duplantis' unwavering passion and extraordinary talent have propelled him to pursue the pole vaulting world record, which has been a distinguishing feature of his career. He was determined to achieve new heights in the sport, as seen by the strategic tactics and concentrated efforts he took along the way to break the world record.

Duplantis started his pursuit of the world record with a string of performances showcasing his developing talent and technical proficiency. His plan included competing in several international events and setting personal bests to gather the momentum needed to challenge the current world record. His strategy comprised not just honing his craft but also comprehending the circumstances and prerequisites required to reach this kind of accomplishment.

He carefully thought out his training regimen to improve his strength, technique, and general performance before making his world record attempts. To increase his chances of shattering the record, Duplantis worked extensively with his trainers to perfect his vaulting technique and maximize his physical state. Because of his preparation, he was able to enter every competition with the assurance and preparedness required to attempt the world record.

Duplantis engaged in several significant competitions in his quest when he nearly broke the record but did not initially succeed. These performances were significant because they gave him insights into what was needed and enabled him to modify his strategy as needed. Every attempt at setting a world record served as a teaching moment that shaped his overarching plan to finally break the record.

Duplantis' performance at the 2021 World Indoor Championships in Belgrade, Serbia, served as the pinnacle of his efforts. He made a determined effort to break the world record at this point. Throughout the tournament, he performed with a distinct emphasis on reaching this objective, making use of all the information and expertise he had accumulated from his earlier attempts. This achievement demonstrated his tenacity and calculated strategy to reach this pole vaulting peak, and it was a significant milestone in his continuous pursuit of the world record.

Duplantis continued to push the limits of the sport and maintained a steady state of high performance during this time. His determination to compete at the top level and push the boundaries of pole vaulting was evident in his systematic and laser-like commitment to his work. To break the world record, he carefully balanced training, competition, and strategic planning at every turn in his quest.

Mondo When Duplantis executed what many regard to be the "perfect vault," a feat of extraordinary technical skill and athleticism, his quest to break the world record in pole vaulting reached a major high point. This is the result of his painstaking preparation and unwavering desire to push the limits of the sport.

Duplantis addressed each effort to break the world record with a determined and deliberate mindset.

Throughout his preparation and competition, he demonstrated his technical accuracy by continuously improving his vaulting technique to get the best results. He spent years honing every facet of his pole vaulting technique and practicing diligently before achieving the perfect vault, which was a crucial component of his quest.

The flawless vault happened in Belgrade, Serbia during the 2021 World Indoor Championships. Duplantis had one specific objective in mind going into this competition: breaking the current world record. He had undergone extensive training in the lead-up to this, covering not just physical but also psychological and technological development.

There were several important elements that marked the execution of the ideal vault. Duplantis demonstrated his extraordinary speed and technique as he sped down the runway with a precise approach to the bar. He was able to maximize the energy transfer into the pole by timing his plant precisely, where the pole makes contact with the takeoff box. After this critical stage, he maneuvered the bend and propulsion of the pole with flawless dexterity.

Duplantis's form demonstrated his technical mastery as he cleared the bar. With perfect alignment and posture, he was able to climb the height with no difficulty. His vault demonstrated his ability to synchronize every action for maximum performance, as evidenced by the extraordinary accuracy with which he timed every move, from takeoff to clearance.

Duplantis' flawless vault demonstrated not only his technical prowess but also his comprehension of the subtleties involved in pole vaulting. His ability to convert his training and preparation into a faultless performance was a noteworthy accomplishment in and of itself. This vault stands out as a pivotal point in his career because it demonstrated his ability to remain composed and perform well in the face of competitive pressure.

Several elements combined to create the flawless vault, including Duplantis' mental toughness, technical proficiency, and physical conditioning. His performance was flawless, demonstrating the intense planning and commitment that went into every aspect of his pole vaulting technique. This was a pivotal point in his quest for the world record and a noteworthy accomplishment for the sport.

Mondo The sports community responded differently to Duplantis' pole vaulting world record leap, which was indicative of the impact the accomplishment had on the sport as well as its importance. His feat, which included shattering the current world record, drew notice from athletes, coaches, and fans worldwide and resulted in a barrage of recognition and appreciation.

Respect and admiration were expressed by competitors and fellow athletes. Many of Duplantis's peers were quick to acknowledge the skill and determination needed to accomplish such a feat, having firsthand experience with the difficulties involved in pole vaulting at the top level. Athletes from all sports and backgrounds recognized the exceptional nature of his accomplishment and applauded his technical execution and the impressive height he cleared.

In their praise, coaches, and sports experts also emphasized the importance of Duplantis' performance in the development of pole vaulting. Pole vaulting coaches who had worked with athletes and watched the sport grow saw that Duplantis' leap set a new standard. They discussed the wider ramifications for training and competition tactics within the sport, emphasizing the painstaking preparation and technical accuracy that went into his achievement.

Commentators and sports experts covered and analyzed Duplantis' record-breaking performance in great detail. Their responses included in-depth analyses of the vault's technical features, including his approach, takeoff, and clearance. Analysts examined the ramifications for the sport's records and competitive standards as well as how his feat showed the possibility for future developments in pole vaulting.

Duplantis' leap received widespread media coverage, with stories and headlines praising his accomplishment. Numerous news organizations worldwide covered the world record's significance, frequently featuring interviews with athletes, coaches, and experts who talked about the performance's effects. The event became the focus of international sports news as a result of the coverage, which emphasized Duplantis' commitment and the extraordinary nature of his accomplishment.

Significantly, pole vaulting enthusiasts and sports fans expressed their admiration and delight for Duplantis' achievement in their replies. Social media was ablaze with fan appreciation for his skill and the historic significance of the leap, as well as discussions and celebrations of his record. Fans' fervor was a reflection of the motivation and excitement Duplantis' performance inspired within the larger athletics community.

His pole vaulting world record leap was an incredible accomplishment that solidified his legacy in the annals of sports history. This incredible achievement marked a turning point for the pole vaulting competition as well as for the individual.

Duplantis broke the previous world indoor record with a leap of 6.19 meters during the 2021 World Indoor Championships in Belgrade, Serbia. The previous world indoor record of 6.18 meters, held by American pole vaulter Sandi Morris, was surpassed by this incredible accomplishment. Duplantis proved he could alter the sport's bounds and push its boundaries by breaking this mark.

To firmly establish his legacy, multiple important elements were engaged. Firstly, Duplantis's world record-breaking feat demonstrated an incredible degree of technical proficiency and physical strength. The dexterity and skill needed to reach that height highlighted his extraordinary athletic ability. In addition to breaking previous marks, the performance demonstrated his creative thinking and technical proficiency in pole vaulting.

Second, the sport has evolved as a result of Duplantis' world record leap. In sports, records are frequently the product of years of advancement and creativity, and Duplantis' success was evidence of this continuous growth. He not only raised the bar for upcoming competitors but also demonstrated the possibility for additional breakthroughs in pole vaulting by achieving a new world record.

Duplantis' world record also had an impact on the entire sporting community worldwide. His accomplishment raised awareness of pole vaulting among athletes and served as an inspiration to others. It emphasized how crucial perseverance and commitment are to attaining sporting success. His accomplishments demonstrated the potential in the sport and provided a baseline for aspiring pole vaulters.

Duplantis' status as one of the best pole vaulters of all time was further cemented by the record. His extraordinary talent and commitment were demonstrated by his ability to smash the world record in a competitive international event. This accomplishment guaranteed that his name would live on in the annals of pole vaulting history, adding to his already impressive collection of honors and solidifying his position as a prominent figure in the sport.

## CHAPTER 7: OLYMPIC GLORY

Mondo Duplantis' rigorous and well-planned preparation for the Tokyo 2020 Olympics demonstrated his dedication to performing at his best on the most prominent sports platform in the world. There were several important components to the preparation, all geared toward making sure he was fit enough to compete successfully in the pole vaulting event.

Duplantis followed a rigorous and targeted training schedule to get ready for the Tokyo Games. His training regimen was created to improve his strength, speed, technique, and general physical fitness, among other performance-related factors. To address the unique needs of pole vaulting, this program combined strength training, endurance training, and technical drills.

A crucial element was technical training, which concentrated on honing his vaulting technique. Work on the vault's approach, plant, and clearance phases was part of this. Duplantis meticulously refined every facet of his technique, collaborating closely with his instructors to guarantee that every move was performed with accuracy. His ability to perform at his best during the competition and attain consistency depended heavily on this thorough technical preparation.

Duplantis' method required mental preparation in addition to physical exercise. The psychological demands of the Olympics required the development of stress management, attention, and mental resilience measures. Duplantis used a variety of mental conditioning tactics, including goal-setting, relaxation exercises, and visualization techniques, to make sure he was psychologically ready for the demands of the Olympic arena.

One aspect of preparation is adjusting to the unique circumstances anticipated during the Tokyo Olympics. Duplantis and his group investigated the environmental elements—such as venue characteristics and weather—that might affect his performance. This allowed him to modify his tactics and technique by practice sessions and simulations created to replicate the environmental factors he would encounter at the Olympics.

Another essential component of his preparation was a clearly defined strategy for competing. This tactic entailed making plans for a variety of eventualities that might occur during the event, such as how to deal with varied elevations and possible rivals. Duplantis and his coaches worked together to create a comprehensive strategy for winning the tournament, one that was modified in response to changing circumstances and other athletes' performances.

Sustaining maximum well-being and overseeing recuperation were essential components of his readiness. Duplantis made sure his body was in top shape for the Games by adhering to a strict health regimen that included relaxation, recuperation methods, and nutrition. He needed to prepare in this way to avoid injuries and make sure he was in peak physical condition for his performance.

A big part of his preparation came from his coaching staff and support personnel. Throughout the training process, the team offered motivation, logistical support, and professional direction. This team effort was crucial to optimizing his performance and making sure that all of his training was in line with his Olympic objectives.

Mondo An important turning point in Duplantis' career came when he competed on the biggest sporting stage in the world—the Tokyo 2020 Olympics. His talents and preparation were put to the test to an unprecedented degree by the distinct opportunities and challenges that came with competing in the Olympics.

Duplantis prepared extensively for the Tokyo Olympics in order to meet the unique requirements of competing in such a prestigious competition. To be ready for the Olympics, he had to modify his training and tactics to take into consideration the special atmosphere, intense competition, and importance of the event.

The Olympic Games, where competitors compete in front of a worldwide audience while being closely observed by the media and supporters, are renowned for their intense atmosphere. For Duplantis, this meant taking the stage during the most renowned athletic event in the world. His performance was under additional pressure because of the tense and exciting atmosphere. It took mental toughness in addition to physical preparation to navigate this environment.

The world's best athletes came together to compete in the Olympics, each striving for the highest accolades. Elite pole vaulters, each with their advantages and tactics, competed against Duplantis. Duplantis had to adjust to the changing circumstances of the competition and use his technique with accuracy in order to compete against opponents of such high ability. He was greatly influenced by the level of competition in how he approached and performed during the Games.

In this high-pressure setting, technical proficiency was essential. Duplantis had to adapt to the unique circumstances of the Olympic location while putting the methods and approaches he had perfected during his preparation to use. This involved controlling the approach run, operating the pole vaulting apparatus, and performing the vault under close observation from the rivals. The key to overcoming the obstacles of the Olympic competition was having accuracy and consistency in every facet of the vault performance.

Organizing travel, lodging, and support staff was another logistical challenge that came with competing in the Olympics. To sustain concentration and productivity, it was crucial to make sure that these factors were well-regulated. In order to focus on his competition, Duplantis was able to manage these logistics with the help of his support crew.

The Olympic Games provide a singular emotional and cultural experience as competitors from all backgrounds unite to compete. For Duplantis, this meant embracing the Olympic spirit, mingling with competitors, and taking in the universal companionship that defines the Games. This wider experience gave his competition an additional dimension and increased the total relevance of his involvement.

Mondo A stunning high point in Duplantis' career, his gold medal moment at the Tokyo 2020 Olympics showcased his exceptional pole vaulting skills and the result of his diligent training. This pivotal moment happened in the pole vault final, where Duplantis won the gold medal with an extraordinarily strong performance.

The Olympic Stadium served as a grand stage for the tournament and hosted the pole vault final of the Tokyo 2020 Olympics. Duplantis faced a field of world-class vaulters who were all competing for the top spot after making it to the finals. With the stakes high and the atmosphere tense with expectation, the event garnered a lot of attention.

Duplantis had an amazing blend of strength, focus, and technique during the final. His methodical approach to the vault demonstrated the fruits of his intense training and planning. Approach, takeoff, and clearance, the three main parts of his vault, were all executed perfectly, demonstrating his mastery of the technique.

The feat of Duplantis clearing the height of 6.02 meters was the high point of his performance. His mastery of the pole vaulting method was evident in the speed, power, and skill he used to achieve this clearance. His height was noteworthy because it demonstrated his preparedness and capacity to succeed in the face of extreme pressure during the Olympic final.

At the end of the competition, Duplantis received the gold medal for his efforts. The gold medal represented the apex of his pole vaulting accomplishments and was a concrete outcome of his skill and perseverance. The crowd erupted in cheers as Duplantis' standing as a top athlete in his discipline was acknowledged by the international athletics community.

The customary festivities, which included the national anthem and medal presentation, defined Duplantis' gold medal moment after the competition. For Duplantis, this portion of the event held great significance, since it signified the conclusion of his endeavors and the acknowledgment of his remarkable achievement.

Mondo Duplantis' Olympic victory has had a significant influence on both his career and the pole vaulting community as a whole, especially in light of his performance in the Tokyo 2020 Olympics. His accomplishments in Tokyo not only demonstrated his extraordinary talent but also revealed his viewpoint on the importance of the Olympic Games and his place in them.

Duplantis achieved a significant personal achievement at the Olympics in Tokyo. A gold medal in the Games signified the achievement of years of diligence, planning, and commitment. For Duplantis, the accomplishment meant more than just winning a medal; it was the realization of a lifelong ambition to compete and perform well at the Olympic Games. This individual victory demonstrated the value of tenacity and dedication in achieving the greatest possible athletic performance.

The Olympic triumph had a big effect on Duplantis' professional path. Gaining gold at the Games increased his stature in the sports world and gave him a springboard for more success and chances. His standing as one of the best pole vaulters of his generation was furthered by the experience, which also provided opportunities for him to win more events domestically and abroad.

Duplantis' burgeoning reputation in the pole vaulting community was aided by his Olympic success. His accomplishment at such a prominent event made him a role model for the sporting community and inspired future athletes. Duplantis changed the perception of pole vaulting and inspired aspirants all around the world by establishing a high bar for perfection.

When considering his Olympic achievements, Duplantis frequently stressed the importance of painstaking planning and execution. He recognized that to succeed at the best level, one must possess strong mental fortitude, strategic preparation, and rigorous training. This contemplation emphasized the significance of a thorough preparation strategy and its influence on winning high-stakes contests.

It is impossible to overestimate the cultural and emotional significance of taking home an Olympic gold medal. For Duplantis, it was a powerful confirmation of his commitment to the game. In addition to being a personal objective, the Olympics symbolize a larger cultural and symbolic accomplishment and the height of athletic competition on a worldwide level.

Following his triumph at the Olympics, Duplantis frequently thought back on his hopes and dreams for the future. The triumph in Tokyo gave him the impetus to establish fresh goals and pursue other accomplishments in his professional life. It also provided him with a chance to expand on his Olympic experience and keep making fresh, significant contributions to the sport.

# CHAPTER 8: CHALLENGES AND TRIUMPHS

In addition to his incredible accomplishments, Mondo Duplantis' athletic career has been defined by the difficulties he has encountered, most notably dealing with setbacks and injuries. Despite being intimidating, these challenges have greatly influenced his career and how he approaches the pole vaulting sport.

Any athlete's career is practically guaranteed to include injuries, and Duplantis has faced serious obstacles as a result of them on several occasions. The physical demands on his body are tremendous as a pole vaulter. The sport puts a lot of physical strain on the body because it demands a combination of strength, speed, and precision. Duplantis has endured ailments over the years that have threatened to impede his development and his ability to play at his peak.

The uncertainty that comes with having an injury is one of the hardest things to live with. Injuries for Duplantis meant not just bodily suffering but also the potential of missing out on important tournaments and the interruption of meticulously planned schedules. With every injury came the need to reevaluate his training program, modify his competition calendar, and frequently dedicate significant amounts of time to recovery rather than his passion for the sport.

Injury-related setbacks frequently result in depressing and frustrating moments. Being unable to compete due to injury was especially tough for Duplantis because he is an athlete who is extremely enthusiastic about his sport. These defeats affected him emotionally as much as physically since they halted the momentum he had gained and cast doubt on his ability to continue in the sport.

Recovering after an injury is a lengthy process that takes a lot of patience. This required Duplantis to undergo protracted periods of rehabilitation, collaborate with medical specialists to regain his strength and flexibility, and progressively restore his performance levels. Every injury needed a customized rehabilitation plan that addressed both the immediate healing of the damage and its prevention in the future.

Duplantis had to modify his approach to training and competing as a result of the setbacks he experienced from injury. He needed to become more aware of the cues his body was giving him, knowing when to push himself and when to back off to prevent hurting himself. This cautious approach was crucial to his recovery and readiness to compete at his best upon his return to competition.

Furthermore, Duplantis frequently had injuries at pivotal moments in his career, such as in the run-up to important tournaments. These situations put his capacity to stay focused and determined in the face of difficulty to the test. The difficulty lay not only in getting better physically but also in regaining the competitive advantage needed to succeed at the top levels of pole vaulting.

The assistance of his team, which included coaches, medical personnel, and family, was vital during these ordeals. They gave him the support and direction he needed to successfully traverse the difficult healing process and make sure he didn't lose sight of his long-term objectives despite the short-term failures.

Mondo In addition to demonstrating his incredible talent, Duplantis' path in the pole vaulting world also demonstrates his remarkable mental and physical resilience. As a top athlete, Duplantis has encountered several difficulties that have put his fortitude, concentration, and resolve to the test. His capacity to overcome these obstacles stems from a strong reservoir of resilience that he has developed over many years of commitment to his sport.

A key element in Duplantis' success is his mental toughness. Pole vaulting and being an elite athlete in general have extremely high mental demands. Every competition demands a strong mental game in addition to physical training. Duplantis has proven to have a remarkable capacity for remaining composed under duress, remaining goal-focused, and handling the psychological demands of elite competition. He has been able to handle both the highs and lows of his career thanks to his mental toughness, which includes handling the pressure of expectations and the unavoidable disappointments that come with being a top-tier athlete.

The mental focus needed to do each leap precisely is one of the most difficult parts of pole vaulting. The sport requires intense focus because even the tiniest distraction can lead to an unsuccessful effort or, worse, an injury. Duplantis' capacity to continuously perform at a high level, even in the most stressful situations, is indicative of his mental toughness. His success on the international scene has been largely attributed to his ability to tune out distractions, his dedication to constant growth, and his focus on honing his technique.

Duplantis has additionally demonstrated remarkable physical fortitude. Pole vaulting is an intense sport with high physical demands. To succeed, you need a certain blend of strength, speed, flexibility, and coordination—all of which need to be precisely calibrated. Even though training and competition can take a toll on one's body, Duplantis has shown time and time again that he can both challenge his body to the maximum and recover from the demands of his sport.

For Duplantis, physical resilience entails more than just being able to make it through taxing workouts or recover from a challenging competition. It also entails long-term maintenance of his physical well-being and conditioning. This calls for a well-calibrated training program that balances workout intensity with enough rest and injury prevention. To maintain his top physical state and continue to compete at a high level throughout his career, Duplantis has collaborated extensively with his coaches and medical staff.

Duplantis' capacity to adapt is a crucial component of his physical resilience. To keep ahead of the competition and take advantage of changes in his physique, he has had to modify his training and technique as an athlete. This flexibility is evidence of his keen awareness of his physical limitations and his dedication to always improving his technique in the game. Duplantis has demonstrated an amazing capacity to adjust to the physical demands of pole vaulting, whether it's changing his training schedule to prevent injury or refining his technique to gain an advantage.

His painstaking attention to detail about his diet, sleep patterns, and general well-being is commensurate with his physical resilience. He has prioritized these elements in his daily routine since he is aware of how important they are to his performance. By treating his physical health holistically, he may maintain his strength and fitness throughout time in addition to being able to perform at a high level.

Mondo Duplantis' capacity to overcome great adversity has marked his path to becoming one of the most renowned pole vaulters in the world. His professional journey has not been an easy one, but one filled with many obstacles that have tried his patience, tenacity, and commitment.

In athletics, adversity can take many different forms. Duplantis has experienced mental, emotional, and physical adversity at various points in his career. Early on, he experienced the expectations and difficulties that come with being a rising star as he made the move from a talented young athlete to a professional competitor. A person with lesser resilience may have easily crumbled under these challenges, but Duplantis showed an amazing capacity to rise beyond them.

Living up to his potential in the public and media's eyes was one of the main challenges Duplantis had to overcome. He was hailed as a potential champion from an early age, a title that came with both opportunity and close attention. He was under tremendous pressure to do well at every competition because of the high expectations that were placed on him. This kind of pressure, particularly for a rookie athlete still figuring out his position in the sport, can be intimidating. Duplantis was able to transform the pressure into drive, though, and he used it as fuel to push himself even harder throughout practice and competition.

Handling the physical demands of pole vaulting has been another major obstacle in Duplantis' career. The risk of injury is always present in this activity, making every attempt a potentially dangerous one. Duplantis has had several injuries, some of which could have seriously hampered his professional progress. Such injuries frequently have a protracted and difficult recovery period, needing not only physical healing but also mental toughness to regain form and confidence. Duplantis' tenacity and resolve are demonstrated by his ability to bounce back from these setbacks and reach the pinnacle of his profession.

In addition, he had to deal with the technical difficulties of pole vaulting, which frequently offered roadblocks that could result in disappointment and failure. The sport of pole vaulting requires flawless timing, technique, and physical conditioning. It can be discouraging for any athlete to experience periods of slow growth and delayed results. Nevertheless, Duplantis was able to overcome these technical difficulties because of his perseverance throughout these trying times, his willingness to learn from his errors, and his constant improvement of his technique.

Duplantis had to contend with the challenge of racing against more seasoned athletes who were sometimes physically stronger and had more experience. He was frequently the youngest and least seasoned contestant when he entered international tournaments. Although this discrepancy might have been a major disadvantage,

Duplantis faced these obstacles head-on and learned from them. He observed his rivals, took note of their advantages and disadvantages, and over time honed the technique and style of play that would ultimately distinguish him.

Duplantis' journey to fame included periods of self-doubt and the battle to be optimistic in the face of obstacles. He went through times, like all athletes, when he felt unconfident, whether it was from a bad game, an injury, or the weight of all the expectations. But what set Duplantis apart was his capacity to face these uncertainties head-on, to endure when it appeared like the cards were stacked against him, and to come out stronger on the other side of every setback.

Mondo In addition to his outstanding accomplishments, his pole vaulting career is distinguished by his unwavering quest to push the limits of what is feasible in his sport. He has always aimed to go beyond the bounds of traditional performance, creating new benchmarks and reinventing the essence of what it means to be a pole vaulter.

The drive behind Duplantis' career to consistently raise the pole vault bar is among its most remarkable features. From his early days of setting age-group records to his more recent exploits as a world record holder, this drive has been visible throughout his career. Over his career, Duplantis has been driven by the challenge of surpassing previous achievements. This goal has driven him to consistently improve and develop his methods in addition to smashing records.

One of the main components of Duplantis' strategy for pushing the envelope is his dedication to becoming an expert pole vaulter. The sport of pole vaulting requires flawless execution in all areas, including strength, speed, timing, and technique. Duplantis has put in countless hours honing these components since he understands that even the slightest advancement could result in a higher vault. Raising the bar, both physically and figuratively, has been made possible by his willingness to try out new methods, modify his strategy, and react to shifting circumstances.

Duplantis has not only demonstrated technical proficiency but also pushed the limits of pole vaulting's physical performance. He has dedicated many hours to gaining the power, speed, and agility necessary to accomplish new heights, and his athleticism is unmatched. His ability to continuously compete at the top level and create new marks has been greatly influenced by his commitment to physical fitness. Duplantis knows that to push the limits of the sport, he needs to constantly push his physical limits and accomplish things that have never been done before.

In addition to pursuing personal success, Duplantis' goal of pushing limits serves as an inspiration to other athletes. He has increased the bar for what pole vaulters can do by breaking records and pulling off feats that were previously unthinkable. His accomplishments have inspired other athletes to challenge themselves and set new goals as a result of his success. In this sense, Duplantis is not just a record-breaker but also a pioneer who is influencing how the sport will develop in the future.

One further crucial component of Duplantis' boundary-pushing mindset is his indomitable spirit in the face of failure. After reaching noteworthy achievements, many sportsmen might be happy to rest on their laurels, but Duplantis has always aimed further. His approach to competition, where he frequently sets his eyes on heights that others might think unattainable, demonstrates this commitment. Duplantis sees every attempt as a chance to grow and learn, even in the face of failure, with the ultimate objective of exceeding his prior best.

Duplantis' career serves as evidence that striving for excellence rather than living in one's comfort zone and never stopping is the path to success. With this mentality, he has pushed the limits of what is feasible in pole vaulting, setting records and leaving a lasting impression on the sport. His unwavering dedication to perfection serves as a reminder that real success stems from a readiness to seize opportunities, take calculated chances, and aim for the extraordinary.

# CHAPTER 9: THE LIFE OF A CHAMPION

Mondo Duplantis, who is well-known for smashing records on the pole vault runway, has an interesting and complex life off the track. Duplantis has developed a personal life apart from competition that showcases his wide range of interests and the challenges of being one of the best athletes in the world.

Duplantis' close bond with his family is the foundation of his life off the track. Growing up in a home where athletics was the main focus, Duplantis' family has always been extremely important to him. This bond endures even while he manages the rigors of an international sporting career. He keeps tight links with his family and frequently turns to them for support and grounding despite his rigorous training program and numerous flights for tournaments. His family has always been a dependable and reassuring presence in his life, whether it is helping him overcome obstacles or celebrating successes.

In addition, Duplantis has a wide range of hobbies outside pole vaulting. These activities provide him with a much-needed break from the demanding world of professional sports. For example, one of his loves is music. He enjoys a wide variety of musical genres and frequently uses music to unwind or get motivated before tournaments. He uses his passion for music for more than simply a pastime; it helps him find emotional equilibrium and connect with himself.

Beyond the track, travel plays a key role in Duplantis' life. His participation in international competitions has allowed him to travel to many different nations and experience their diverse cultures and customs. His viewpoint has been widened and his comprehension of the world has been enhanced by these encounters. As an athlete and someone interested in life outside of athletics, Duplantis cherishes these opportunities. He takes the time to discover new locations, frequently combining his travels with leisure pursuits that let him relax and rejuvenate.

He is well-known for enjoying outdoor pursuits. He had a deep connection to nature as a child growing up in Louisiana, and he loves being outside whenever he can. Hiking, fishing, or just taking in the calm and quiet of the outdoors are some of the hobbies that bring him serenity and renewal. The outdoors allows him to decompress and unwind in contrast to the stress of his pole vaulting career.

Even though he is well-known, he still enjoys hanging out with friends and participating in social events unrelated to pole vaulting. He values keeping these relationships because they give him a window into the world outside of professional athletics. Going out to eat, going to events, or just hanging around are examples of activities that keep him centered and linked to a more typical, everyday existence.

Duplantis' style and sense of fashion are apparent in the way he conducts himself both on and off the track. He has a good sense of style and likes to try out new outfits. He frequently incorporates aspects of his style into his public appearances. Apart from his identity as an athlete, this passion for fashion is another method for him to express his uniqueness and originality.

Mondo Duplantis, a well-known athlete, has the particular problem of striking a balance between his need for solitude and notoriety. Due to his quick ascent to fame in the pole vaulting community, he is now well-known and frequently the focus of intense scrutiny in both his personal and professional lives. It takes careful navigation to manage this fame while preserving privacy.

After setting numerous world records and winning an Olympic gold medal, Duplantis's notoriety skyrocketed. He consequently rose to prominence as a global sports icon, drawing interest from sponsors, media, and supporters. This degree of celebrity comes with pressures as well as opportunities. Duplantis must deal with the loss of his anonymity and the ongoing attention that his life receives from the public while simultaneously having the platform to inspire and impact millions of people.

Setting boundaries between his public and private lives is necessary to strike a balance between his popularity and privacy. Duplantis has taken great care to maintain his privacy, keeping everything unrelated to his sport out of his public domain. By using this strategy, he can preserve his feeling of normalcy and shield his intimate relationships and experiences from prying eyes.

Duplantis must exercise caution while interacting with the media and his fan base to manage his notoriety. Despite his reputation for professionalism and warmth, he knows how important it is to maintain control over the story that is told about him. To avoid feeling overburdened by the pressures of celebrity, he must exercise discretion in what information he reveals and when he appears in public.

Duplantis handles the difficulties of social media, where sportsmen are frequently expected to stay active these days. Social media gives him a direct channel of communication with his followers, but it also exposes his life to criticism and public debate. Duplantis maintains a tight eye on his social media presence, balancing interaction with his followers with protecting his privacy.

Mondo Duplantis has inspired the next generation of athletes and young people worldwide with his extraordinary accomplishments and qualities. His transformation from a talented teenage athlete to a world champion and record holder has struck a deep chord, especially with aspiring pole vaulters and sports fans who view him as an inspiration for greatness, commitment, and enthusiasm.

The influence of Duplantis on the younger generation is complex. First of all, his early success demonstrates that anyone can excel in any sport at any level given talent, dedication, and the correct resources. This is particularly effective in pole vaulting, a sport that calls for technical accuracy, mental toughness, and physical strength in addition to physical strength. Duplantis serves as an inspiration to young athletes, showing them that hard work and a determination to push boundaries may lead to greatness.

Duplantis motivates others in addition to his athletic ability by exemplifying humility and sportsmanship. Even though he's one of the best sportsmen in the world, he manages to stay humble and friendly. Young fans are especially affected by this kind of behavior because they perceive him as a hero who still values honesty, decency, and respect. Duplantis's contacts with fans—especially the younger ones—show that he is aware of his influence and that he wants to make the most of it.

Through his commitment to the sport of pole vaulting, Duplantis also serves as an inspiration to the future generation. Even after reaching significant milestones, his dedication to honing his art sends a strong message about the value of constant progress and the pursuit of perfection. Young athletes are inspired to pursue their training with the same amount of passion and determination after witnessing Duplantis' unwavering work ethic.

Being a hybrid of Swedish and American cultures, his success story appeals to youth all around the world. His ability to succeed internationally while bridging cultural divides emphasizes the value of variety and embracing one's roots. This facet of his identity establishes his relatability to a broad audience and proves that excellence is not limited to a certain background or nation.

His openness to sharing his achievements, struggles, and experiences with the world teaches future athletes important lessons. He offers insight into the realities of seeking athletic achievement, including the sacrifices, the hard work, and the mental fortitude needed to overcome difficulties, by candidly sharing the highs and lows of his career. Young athletes benefit from this candor by learning that failures are a necessary part of the process and that persistence is essential for success on their journeys.

Mondo Duplantis has a bright future ahead of him filled with endless possibilities and sustained success in the sports world. Duplantis is a young athlete who has accomplished a great deal, and he is well-positioned to influence the sport's future and possibly even alter its boundaries.

Duplantis's capacity to keep pushing pole vaulting's limits is one of the important components of his future. Duplantis is in a unique position to significantly raise the bar for the sport, having already established many world records. He may continue to break new ground and set even greater marks that could last for decades because of his technical skill and creative approach to training and competition.

Duplantis' experience will be invaluable in his future pursuits as he develops as a person and as an athlete. He will apply the knowledge gained from his early career's triumphs and setbacks to his attitude to training, competition, and even off-field pursuits. His development is expected to enhance his athletic prowess and elevate his stature in the sports world.

He may go on to receive more honors and recognition on a global scale in the future. There are plenty of opportunities for him to add to his already outstanding list of accomplishments as long as he competes at the highest levels. Duplantis can achieve major championships, world titles, and possibly even more Olympic gold medals, securing his place among the best pole vaulters of all time.

Duplantis' future may involve more than just pole vaulting; it might also involve extending his influence in other areas. Duplantis can influence a larger audience with endorsements, speeches, or even projects about youth involvement and sports development. As a world champion, he has the platform to inspire people outside of the sports world and to speak up for causes that he supports.

For Duplantis to continue, as with any elite athlete, he will need to remain in top physical and mental shape. The rigors of elite sports necessitate ongoing focus on well-being, fitness, and health. The future performance of Duplantis will be determined by his ability to handle the wearisome obstacles that come with a protracted career in athletics, including weariness, injuries, and the psychological toll of persistent competition.

Mondo Duplantis' changing legacy will probably define his future. His impact on the pole vaulting sport will increase as he achieves more and motivates others. In addition to his accomplishments and records, upcoming generations of athletes will hold him in high regard for his behavior throughout his career. Duplantis' legacy will be one of creativity, quality, and the unwavering quest for greatness, acting as a role model for his successors.

# CHAPTER 10: LEGACY IN THE MAKING

Even thus early in his career, he has already had a significant impact on the pole vaulting sport. His influence on the discipline goes beyond the heights he has attained and includes how coaches and athletes alike view, approach, and engage with the sport.

Duplantis' combination of athleticism and skill has had a major influence on pole vaulting, raising the bar for what is considered achievable in the sport. Pole vaulters now practice and compete differently as a result of their ability to regularly produce high marks with a style that combines speed, agility, and technical accuracy. Now, more athletes and coaches are focusing on the subtleties of Duplantis' technique, from takeoff to bar clearance. This has increased interest in improving the sport's technical features and raised the bar for competition across the globe.

Pole vaulting has also gained popularity again as a result of Duplantis' achievement, especially among younger audiences. Pole vaulting has become more popular and approachable thanks to his captivating performances and obvious love for the sport, attracting more followers and competitors. For a sport that has long been recognized but frequently existed in the shadow of more popular athletics, this return of interest is essential. Pole vaulting has become more popular thanks to Duplantis' personality and public-facing skills, which will assist ensure that it receives the recognition it merits.

Duplantis has not only stimulated interest from onlookers but also innovation in the sport. His training philosophy, which combines old and modern methods, has encouraged other athletes and coaches to push the envelope and try new things. Pole vaulting as a discipline needs to be open to innovation to continue developing since it creates new opportunities for performance enhancement and the exploration of human potential.

Duplantis' influence can also be seen in how people today perceive and handle competition. Fans and other competitors alike understand that when they see him at an event, they are watching someone who is not just competing but also influencing the sport's future, which adds to the thrill and expectation. Pole vaulting competitions now hold a higher status and are main draws at important athletic events as a result.

Due to Duplantis' accomplishments, pole vaulting has seen a rise in funding. Because of the sport's potential for expansion and attractiveness to a worldwide audience, sponsors and sports organizations are now more eager to support and promote it. This investment is essential to the pole vaulting sport's future development since it provides the funds required to improve training facilities, find new talent, and host more competitive events.

Mondo Duplantis has pushed pole vaulting to new heights, breaking records that were previously unthinkable. His approach to the game combines a remarkable combination of mental tenacity, technical ingenuity, and physical talent, which enables him to push the envelope in ways that very few people have done before him.

Duplantis' unwavering quest for perfection is among the most important ways he has changed the sport. He has continuously cleared heights that few thought were possible, raising the bar both literally and figuratively. His world record leaps are more than just assessments of his physical prowess; they signify a change in the pole vaulting community's overall perspective. Duplantis has broken through barriers that previously appeared unbreakable, creating room for new records and encouraging others to think that everything is possible.

The way Duplantis redefines the sport also greatly depends on his technique. His technique is a masterclass in how to blend strength, quickness, and accuracy. His plant is extremely powerful, his run-up is faster than most, and his ability to controllably bend his body over the bar is nothing short of revolutionary. As a result, coaches and athletes alike are reevaluating training regimens and approaches within the sport to imitate and learn from Duplantis' methodology.

Furthermore, Duplantis' success has led to modifications in the format and evaluation system of competitions. His ability to routinely clear high bars has sparked conversations about how to keep the sport challenging even as athletes achieve ever-higher feats. This involves prospective changes to competition formats, records recognition, and pole vaulting equipment to keep up with the new benchmarks Duplantis has established.

Beyond simply his accomplishments, his impact has spurred a surge of innovation in pole vaulting equipment. Manufacturers are looking to Duplantis as a catalyst for innovations that could provide athletes an advantage in reaching higher altitudes, from the poles themselves to the shoes worn by athletes. This emphasis on innovation is essential to the development of the sport since it drives players and the gear they use to always improve.

Duplantis has redefined the sport's bounds and changed notions of what a pole vaulter can accomplish in a career. In the past, becoming the pinnacle of the sport could have required clearing a specific height or taking home a big title. The concept of success has been broadened, with Duplantis serving as the standard. These days, athletes have larger goals in mind, both for the heights they want to reach and the records they want to shatter. Duplantis' influence is directly responsible for this change in goal.

Mondo As an athlete, Duplantis has gained a lot of influence since he embodies values and traits that inspire great admiration in those who look up to him. His transformation from a young, gifted vaulter to a professional athlete provides insightful knowledge and motivation for upcoming competitors.

Duplantis' popularity as a role model is mostly attributed to his commitment to his sport. His unwavering dedication to training, meticulous nature, and unwavering work ethic are the epitome of what it takes to succeed at the top. Duplantis exemplifies the value of persistence and tenacity by constantly pushing himself to do better and aim for excellence. Young athletes are inspired to approach their own training and ambitions with a similar level of dedication after witnessing them get the benefits of perseverance.

He also inspires me with the way he approaches competition. Athletes aspire to be like Duplantis because of his ability to perform well under duress and his resilience in high-pressure situations. His ability to perform well in important competitions under severe strain is a compelling example of how to manage the psychological demands of athletics. Young athletes are inspired by this facet of their career to cultivate mental toughness and maintain self-assurance in their skills.

Duplantis' humility and good sportsmanship also make him an inspiration. Even with his impressive accomplishments, he keeps a humble demeanor and respects his rivals. His graciousness in winning and losing emphasizes how important it is to have a positive outlook and treat others with respect. This behavior establishes a benchmark for young athletes, highlighting the fact that success in sports involves not just individual accomplishment but also social interactions with fellow competitors.

Duplantis' success in a variety of settings, including playing against a wide range of rivals and competing in other nations, highlights the need for flexibility and openness. Young athletes are motivated by their versatility and willingness to take on new challenges when it comes to their training and competitive mindset. It emphasizes the notion that success frequently necessitates adjusting to various circumstances and picking up knowledge from a variety of experiences.

The significance of intensely pursuing one's passion is further highlighted by Duplantis' story. His transformation from an eager adolescent vaulter to the holder of a world record demonstrates how passion and dedication can result in incredible achievements. Aspiring athletes can relate to this zeal and are inspired to pursue their own goals with similar fervor and determination.

Looking ahead, several significant events and turning points that could further mold Mondo Duplantis' legacy are expected to occur. His next moves will probably consist of a mix of pushing pole vaulting boundaries further, taking on new challenges, and making an impact outside of the sport.

To keep up his supremacy in the pole vaulting world, Duplantis plans to improve his technique and set new world records. As an athlete, he might experiment with new methods and ideas to improve his performance. His continuous pursuit of greatness will not only cement his place in the sport's history but also establish new benchmarks for vaulters in the future.

Duplantis plans to compete in more important athletics competitions shortly, including as World Championships, Diamond League meets, and maybe the Olympic Games. Every tournament offers him the chance to show off his abilities and even set new records, solidifying his reputation as the sport's dominant force.

Pole vaulting is likely to change as a result of Duplantis' achievements and innovations. His strategies, approaches to training, and competitive demeanor may influence changes in the way the sport is perceived and played. Technological and instructional developments in pole vaulting may result from this effect.

Duplantis might become more involved in public events such as motivational speaking, endorsements, and community outreach in addition to his sporting endeavors. He can benefit the larger sports community and encourage more young athletes by making the most of his position.

Personal development for Duplantis will also be a part of his journey; this will include learning new abilities as a leader, pursuing interests outside of pole vaulting, and possibly discovering new interests. His accomplishments and experiences will probably open up new doors for him in the sports industry as well as outside of it.

He may participate in projects that help youth development initiatives or give back to the sport. His legacy may include initiatives like building training centers, sponsoring grassroots pole vaulting programs, or advancing sports education.

# CONCLUSION

As "Mondo Duplantis' Athletic Journey: Flying to Glory" comes to an end, we are left with a great deal of appreciation for the remarkable career that Mondo Duplantis has made for himself in the pole vaulting world. His narrative is the tale of a young athlete who has redefined what is possible in his sport, not only the records he has broken or the medals he has won.

The transformation of Duplantis from a gifted teenage vaulter to an international star is evidence of his extraordinary combination of innate skill, unwavering dedication, and passion for pole vaulting. His accomplishments, which include breaking world records and winning gold at the Olympics, highlight a career characterized by ground-breaking success as well as a strong dedication to pushing the sport's limits. Every leap he has made is a result of his creative thinking, careful planning, selflessness, and perseverance, not just a physical accomplishment.

Duplantis has taught us priceless lessons about tenacity, concentration, and the value of accepting difficulties throughout his career. His capacity for excellence under duress and his unwavering commitment to self-improvement provide a success formula that transcends the realm of sports. Anybody hoping to succeed in their endeavors, regardless of the sector, can find inspiration from these insights into his approach to training, competition, and personal development.

Mondo Duplantis' journey serves as a testament to the value of cooperation and assistance. His accomplishments are closely linked to the support and direction he received from his mentors, coaches, and family. Their contributions have been crucial to his growth, emphasizing the teamwork required for achievement and the value of having a solid support network when striving for greatness.

Mondo Duplantis is well-positioned to carry on having a big influence on pole vaulting and the larger sports world as we move to the future. His impact will probably have a lasting effect on the development of the sport, motivating upcoming vaulters and propelling improvements in gear and technique. With Duplantis leading the way, pole vaulting has a bright future filled with increased innovation and improved standards.

The book "Mondo Duplantis' Athletic Journey: Flying to Glory" is more than just an account of his incredible sporting accomplishments. It honors a path filled with commitment, development, and a significant influence on the pole vaulting sport. The inspirational tale of Duplantis shows the amazing heights that can be attained with tenacity and desire. At the end of this chapter, we are reminded of the enduring legacy Duplantis is building and the exciting future he and the sport he continues to elevate have in store.

Printed in Great Britain
by Amazon